# Mendeleev's Mandala

# Mendeleev's Mandala

## Poems by Jessica Goodfellow

Mayapple Press 2015

Published by    MAYAPPLE PRESS
                362 Chestnut Hill Road
                Woodstock, NY 12498
                *www.mayapplepress.com*

ISBN: 978-1-936419-49-4
Library of Congress Control Number: 2014958299

ACKNOWLEDGMENTS

Grateful acknowledgment is made to the editors of the following journals, in which some
of these poems, in some cases in earlier versions, first appeared, or will soon appear:

*Arch Literary Journal, Barrow Street, Beloit Poetry Journal, Black Tongue Review, Boxcar Poetry
Review, Cellpoems, Copper Nickel, diode, Eleven Eleven Literary Journal, Emrys Journal, Filter
Literary Journal, Forklift, Ohio: A Journal of Poetry, Cooking & Light Industrial Safety, Hunger
Mountain, Motionpoems, Ninth Letter Arts & Literary Journal, Passages North, Phoebe: A Journal of
Literature and Art, Thrush Poetry Journal, Turk's Head Review, Vinyl Poetry.*

Several poems were published in the chapbook, *A Pilgrim's Guide to Chaos in the Heartland*
(Concrete Wolf, 2006).

Cover by Judith Kerman based on diatom photo by Rehemat Bhatia, used under Creative
Commons Attribution 3.0 Unported. The image color has been inverted. Text design
and layout by Judith Kerman and Amee Schmidt in Perpetua with Candara titles. Author
photo by Janne Rytkonen.

# Contents

## one

## two

# three

# four

# five

for my siblings: J, J, S, J, J, J, & J

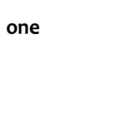

**one**

# The Problem with Pilgrims

The problem with pilgrims is they think words are souvenirs.

The problem with pilgrims is, though they haven't been here before, they insist everything has been picked *up* and placed *down* a quarter inch to the left of where it used to be.

The problem with pilgrims is they ask questions that make your sisters cry but when you move in closer, everyone falls silent.

The problem with pilgrims is they have forgotten *taboo* means not only *forbidden* but also *holy*.

The problem with pilgrims is, when you tell them nothing has been lifted *up* and placed *down* a quarter inch to the left—it's just a visual illusion of forgiveness—they smile as if they don't believe you, and then forgive you for your lie. When they walk out the door, everything slides another quarter inch left.

The problem with pilgrims is each one pockets a stone when he thinks no one is looking. Or a shell. Or a sister.

The problem with pilgrims is they have no fixed coordinates. They leave their blackened hats on your dining room chairs and no forwarding address except a latitude. Never a longitude, as they are only concerned with relative placement *up* and *down*, not left and right.

The problem with pilgrims is they can go home, but you already are.

. . .  . . .  . . .  . . .  . . .  . . .  . . .  . . .  . . .

If you could say only one word for the remainder of your life, what would it be?

You'd say, *Bone. Bone.* No, *gravity. Gravity* is the word you would choose.

The pilgrims exchange amused glances. Somehow you have failed, which hurts you. *Broken*, you suggest. *Icicle*, you hazard. *Echo. Equinox. Counterexample.*

The pilgrims' rules include you being the only one subject to their restrictions. Also, you cannot explain to the others in any way why you keep repeating one word, except to say the word again. *Fossil. Ellipsis. Archipelago.*

You watch them walk away, their shaggy haircuts standing in for hair shirts, less scruffy than your jacket worn four winters now. *Forgive*, you call after them. *Forgiven.* They turn, shrug slightly, and keep walking. *Away.*

The problem with pilgrims is they think you are apologizing.

. . .          . . .          . . .

. . .                    . . .                    . . .

. . .          . . .          . . .

God let Adam name the beasts of the Earth.
In turn, Adam let Eve name the long-legged birds
he'd seen her watching, with their built-in
backup plans. He *let* her.
How did he think he could stop her? Still,
somehow the fact of his listening
perplexed her so that she gave them
names sounding only close to what
she had wanted to say: *egret, bittern, crane.*

The pilgrims must have let your sisters name something.

. . .          . . .          . . .

. . .          . . .          . . .

. . .                              . . .

Due to continental drift, the place a fossil is uncovered is often not where the Earth first swaddled it. Fossils and rocks have no words: you cannot ask them. However, if studded with iron-rich particles, a fossil or rock will align magnetically, like a compass point, with the latitude of where it was formed, not with where it wandered. Or was wandered. The problem with pilgrims is they pretend not to know this.

The problem with pilgrims is long after you've banished them from the colony, you are still wondering: *Tundra. Artifact. Subtract.*

The problem with pilgrims is they don't entertain counterexamples.

*Counterexample:* Too late you realize the pilgrims were ripening you for the flight of your sisters, so after loss you would not be surprised to find any word as wanting as any other. *Other.*

Study of iron-rich particles in rocks and fossils also reveals that the magnetism of the Earth has reversed numerous times in the past, North Pole becoming South, and vice versa. It is you who pretend not to know this.

You, who use too many words to say simply *Wait*.

The problem with pilgrims is they have not noticed that *chants* sounds the same as *chance*.

At night you dream of the Uncertain Archipelago—lonely string of fossil-studded islands, together in a geology of solitude. When you wake you pack your rucksack, depart the colony, knowing you must not stop until you find them.

The problem with pilgrims is now you are one. *Egret. Bittern. Crane.*

. . .

       . . .       . . .

. . .       . . .

    . . .

        . . .

     . . .

# Crows, Reckoning

A crow remembers who crowded it out of the trash can,
who cast at it sticks and rocks and rockets fashioned from bottles.
Long after you have forgotten, the crow remembers your face,
the space between your eyes, the rise of your cheek,
your beakless maw, and with caw both credo and cri de coeur,
the crow causes you to recall that gardens are, by their nature,
not nature, but the cult of cranium over creation,
a human rebuke cloaked in clover and cockscomb and crocus.
A crow says, If a garden is not god-wrung, then who
seeded the Garden of Eden, crux of the human cradle,
till ceded by Adam and even then who, do you suppose,
forespoke the stain of Cain if not a crow, or a murder
of crows.

# Imagine No Apples

*All beginnings wear their endings like dark shadows.*
　　　—Chet Raymo, astronomer-physicist

All beginnings wear their endings like dark apples.
A is for apple. B is not for apple.
C, also not for apple. And so on.
Everything always ends up apple, or not apple.
Pick any beginning and there's the apple,
never falling far enough from the tree:
the apple and the omega.

All beginnings wear their apples like dark shadows.
For example, Eve in the Garden
stood beneath the Tree of Knowledge,
biting into forbidden fruit.
Beguiled but enlightened, sated and falling
she dragged all humanity with her by bruised heels—
suddenly everyone banished from paradise.

All apples wear their shadows like dark endings.
For example, Newton in the garden
dozed beneath a tree, dreamt of seeking knowledge,
awoke to see a red globe falling.
Drowsy but enlightened with heaviness,
he saw one sad secret of the universe revealed—
suddenly everyone stuck to this planet.

All dark shadows wear their endings like beginnings.
But suppose not. Imagine no apples:
everyone still naked; all of physics stymied.
No one to say *Oh, this is gravity*,
or *Ah, this is sin*.
Would we be better off, would we be happier,
sinless and floating, or if not actually floating,
still capable of hoping to rise.

# Mendeleev's Mandala

A house afire, or rather
    his mother's glass factory, actually,
        and under the smolder the child Dmitri
            understood that he would reject the 4 elements
                of water, earth, air, and fire to insist on an order
                    no one else noticed, like a secret 27th letter of
                        the alphabet, a chemical koan. It would take
                            many train rides, his flesh (carbon, hydrogen,

phosphorous) pressed to the window (silicon,
    oxygen) before he could dream chemistry
        out of chaos and into a grid, and with the gall
            of gallium, leave    spaces    for what was still
                missing. What less could he do, a boy who saw
                    his father go blind, his mother lose everything, a
                      child whose siblings numbered maybe 13, perhaps
                        14, no one knew which (but the sum is the secret

27), number of the element cobalt, which
    Mendeleev in his table (less manual than mandala)
        switched with nickel, seeing, despite atomic weight,
            to which family it truly belonged. Once he'd deci-
                phered the hidden matrix of matter, codex for the elixir
                    of existence, once he'd proven there are no spare parts,
                        he set out to show it's *all* spare parts. For refusing
                        haircuts and trimmed beards, for riding with the

peasants in 3rd class, for marrying 2 women
    at once, even the czar forgave him. The chaos
        he'd once chastened he now chased, his own
            odyssey of periodicity, a conservation of
                confusion. A mind this aligned must be
                ransomed by entropy eventually: every fact/
                    (ory) is finally equal parts glass, equal parts
                      fire, which is to say: all fire, all beginnings.

# The Mother of Nations Waits

Sarai, the Baroness of Barrenness,
the woman with a womb like a memory like a sieve,
sent a valentine to Wittgenstein, a poem to Plotinus,
a letter to Leibniz, inventor of the binary code.
Across the bottom of the pages, in lieu of $X$'s and $O$'s,
she scrawled strings of ones and zeros,
promises of everything and nothing,
and nothing in between.
(Not one answered.)

In the time before zeros
merchants marked nothing with nothing,
leaving spaces to show where something was missing.
But what shape was the space?
Sarai wanted to know, pressing on her midriff,
hoping that containing the emptiness
was a possibility.

And then there *were* zeros, just like that!
From Babylon came symbols whose presence
meant the absence of everything else.
All losses were made equal,
which was a relief to Sarai
and which wasn't.

Later Leibniz would spin whole worlds
out of ones and zeros
but what can you make from only zeros?
Whatever you add, that's still all you've got
and maybe you've lost yourself for the effort.
You can't be a little bit pregnant.

Abraham called to Sarai, husband of her broken heart,
but she was bent over a mathematics text,
muttering in not-yet-invented codes
(zeros and ones, eggs and sperm)
and she didn't hear.

Isaac called to her, son of her broken womb,
and she could not hear; an angel and a ram rescued him instead.

Or she heard, but could not believe she had heard.
Because while the opposite of being fertile is being barren,
the opposite of being barren is still being barren.

# If-Then, Iphigenia

An *if-then* statement is called a *conditional*: If A, Iphigenia, then B.
For example: If a father loves his daughter, then he does not kill her.
If this statement is true, then a father's love for his daughter is said to be a *sufficient condition* for him not to kill her.
If this statement is true, then that a father does not kill his daughter is a *necessary condition* for his love.

*Converse Statement:* If, Iphigenia, B, then A.
For example, the *converse* of the example statement is: If a father does not kill his daughter, then he loves her.
The *converse* may or may not be true, even if the original statement is true, which has not yet been established in this case.

Iphigenia puts down her pen. She thinks of Abraham and Isaac, that other story, how differently logic functions when *daughter* is replaced with *son*.

*Contrapositive:* If not B, Iphigenia, then not A.
For example, the *contrapositive* of our original statement is: If a father kills his daughter, then he does not love her.
This is logically equivalent to the original statement, meaning that the original statement and the *contrapositive* must both be true or must both be false, neither of which has yet been established in this case.

It's only a story, Iphigenia's father tells her. You are a stochastic stoic, and your life is only a story.
What about Isaac, wonders Iphigenia, and his story, hisstory, history?

*Inverse Statement:* If not A, then, Iphigenia, not B.
For example, the *inverse* of our original statement is: If a father does not love his daughter, then he kills her.
The *inverse* is the *contrapositive* of the *converse*, which means it may or may not be true, even if the original statement (and therefore the *contrapositive*) is true, which has not yet been established in this case,
but if the *converse* is true, then the *inverse* must also be true, which has still not been established in this case.

Iphigenia notices that both her name and Isaac's start with the letter *I*.
Coincidence, this annihilation of the *I*? Of the *eye*? But Isaac survives. The masculine *I* is not sacrificed. Or the masculine *eye*.

Iphigenia's mother reminds her that in some versions of her story she is rescued. By a goddess. By Artemis, virgin of the hunt, the same goddess her father first offended. And she, Iphigenia, is replaced at the sacrificial altar by a stag, a bloody deer. Alter(ed) by a bloody deer, a bloody dear. A disguise. Disguise->disguys->disg(eyes).

In Isaac's story too, he is replaced at the altar, thinks Iphigenia, with a ram from a thicket. From the thick of the thicket came a ram to stand in for a son. For Isaac. For his eye. His e – y (chromosome) – e. His *I*.

In the pocket of her tunic, Iphigenia fingers a missive she received from Isaac, revealing the *Law of the Altar / Law of the Alter(ed)*:
If there is a female god, then a female sacrifice is required.
If a male god, then a male sacrifice.

The sacrifice must be in the image, in the eye, in the *I* of the god, replies Iphigenia. What does this mean?
It means, returns Isaac, that the solution to our problems, the secret to our survival, is to swap identities. Or else, to swap gods.

This seems to Iphigenia an unlikely scenario.
Isaac's father Abraham surely would not allow it.
Her father Agamemnon surely would not allow it.
Surely no father whose name starts with the letter *A*, the alpha letter, would allow it.
Instead Iphigenia reckons the *contrapositive*, which, if the law cited by Isaac is true, must also be true:
If not a female sacrifice, then not a female god.
If no male sacrifice, then no male god.
And in their stories, hers and Isaac's, there is no male sacrifice. That much, at least, has been established in these cases.

When Agamemnon intercepts Iphigenia's next note, Isaac never again hears from his friend, his dear, deer friend. He never stops wondering why, y (chromosome), why. And why the wind seems to follow him everywhere and always, a wind he doesn't recognize as the one Iphigenia's father traded her for, ten thousand invisible fingers, an ever-open palm holding nothing.

It is this same wind that parts the leaves in the thicket, revealing the ram with which Isaac's father replaces him at the altar, giving credit to a male god, the altar's truth, the alter(ed) truth.

One day Iphigenia's father writes a letter to Isaac's father. There is no record of what it says. Isaac's father never answers. In fact he never receives the letter. It is carried away in a sudden gust of wind. And, like a god, never seen again. By any eye, *I*, aye.

# How to Find a Missing Father in a Town that Isn't There

The town where my father was born
was long ago swallowed up
by the copper mine it was birthed to serve:
my first first-hand experience of a parent
eating his child. Since we could not visit
the town, we stood instead at the edge
of a nearly-mile-deep pit, watching trucks
corkscrew the walls until they disappeared,
like my father's father who'd worked one season here.
*Mine*, my father joked, pointing into the gaping hole.
*Not mine*, he waved his arms in large gestures
in no particular direction. To distract him
I read aloud, *Used anciently to make mirrors.*
He nodded, *The sheathing on the hulls
of the Pinta, the Nina, the Santa Maria.*
*The Statue*, we said in unison, *of Liberty.*

Before we left I bought myself
at the mine gift shop a ring, a copper band
of hearts that turned my finger green
and soon snapped in two. I handed one half to my father,
tossed the other into the pit, losing sight of it
before it hit its lineage. When he pocketed his piece,
I frowned, but my father shrugged, and said,
*Semiconductor chips and tea carts.*
I nodded, *Coat trees and undersea cables.*
*Saxophones, stained glass, and pacemakers.*
I did not mean to mean the mine was a mirror
or vice versa. What I should have said was
*Lightning rod*, something needed, in theory, only once.
Like a father. Which may be of scant comfort,
or untrue, as any gauge that measures the depths of the pit
is likely made itself of copper.

# Pittsburgh Stories

the/a  woman/crow  who/that  said/cried  fertility/nothing  sounds/begets
                            like/more  futility/nothing;


            asleep                                      finger;
the         burnished        on a north-facing          penny;
a           moon             dark as an heiress's
            boy


a
that        woman
            stone        waiting
                         yet            to stop
                                        interrupting        waiting;
                                                            dirt;


                                                    fog;
                                        of          hope;
                            lithograph  via
                            execution
                in a(n)     's final
blind man
one         son
only


only if  | a vague       | regret is | less bearable than    | a precise    | regret.
if only  | one person's  | story is  | interchangeable with  | a stranger's | story.

19

# The Factory

These were her father's last words: "I have a dread of chaos in my heart."
Or, "I have a dread of *the* chaos in my heart." The two others present—
her mother, her brother—and she later cannot agree. It was perhaps

a critique of the cryptic vehicles of concealment—symmetry and white noise,
city blocks and hinterlands—she thinks now, as she watches her son watch
a praying mantis watch a caterpillar. The caterpillar is famously playing

dead. Suddenly she wonders if her father is watching her
watching her son watching the praying mantis watching the caterpillar
playing dead. Windows within windows within something window-shaped.

*Kilroy was here* means he's not anymore—a kind of geometry nobody
cannot configure. She imagines her father working, somewhere, in a factory
that churns out checkerboards, one after another, black and red,

ordinate and abscissa, drawing the axis between *obsess* and *abyss*.
Confess and confuse: there is a blind spot in her blind spot in the shape of
a heart in chaos, *or* chaos in a heart, red on black, *or* vice versa.

# Wilbur Wright Consults a Fortune Teller

What cannot be fashioned from spruce,
muslin and roller skate wheels may not be
worth making. Also you will never marry.
Lift and rise are, like you and your brother,
as close to twins as to opposites, a wing
that casts two shadows. Remember: twine
should be waxed. With it you will build the world
a better trapeze—bodies vaulting past clouds
the color of bone, through a blue-hued fenestra,
a blooming absence of fence. Bamboo, paper,

and cork I see fastened with a rubber band.
Refuser of roofs, you were born *afflicted*
*with the belief that flight is possible,* cursed
with the hope of a mobile Babel above
the horizon's scaffold, a solitary vision
of soaring in you like a sore. You who confuse
departure with arrival rival only swallows
and eagles—creatures wound around hollow
skeletons. The migration of cranes makes you
dizzy and giddy and grief-bound. Never mind:

*no bird soars in a calm.* In your future I see
travel: Italy, Germany and many times France
where they have different words for rivers
that run to the sea and rivers that don't.
Pay attention: wind is the river of the sky,
with nothing more known of its dispatch
of absence. Beware: the right wing must stretch
four inches farther than the left, a counterbalance
for what you must carry that ticks and hums,
sputters and dies. The promise your father made you

make is meaningless; when the time comes
*gravity will have served you no better*
*than a balky horse.* The universe is nothing
if not counterbalanced: wind can move anything,
an angel can do anything, and a man can have anything
done to him. *There is no flying art, but only*
*a flying problem,* sometimes *solved with two wings*

*at different angles to the wind.* Grounded, you will watch
your brother subdue the stratosphere, upending the impossible,
paying for the *art of equilibrium* with reckless loss.

# The Soul Solution

*Your soul*, the guru said, *is a concentrated point*
*of light, here in the center of your forehead.*
This was news to me who had supposed my soul to be
a sort of cut-out shadow of my lumpy body,
a paper-doll torso, only more so, minus the paper.

*Not so*, the guru said as she began to fade away right there
in front of my eyes, or what I've always taken to be my eyes.
*Don't leave me here alone*, I cried, *with my puny soul.*
*You're not*, I heard her say though I could no longer see her,
and what I expected to hear next was *alone, you're not alone.*

But what she said was *here, you're not here.* I have my doubts
but let's suppose the guru's right and I'm not here and my soul's
a concentrated point of light. But if I'm not here then neither is
my forehead. Yoohoo, see-through guru, wherever it is you are,
who's to say my soul's not a miasma of plasma? Or electron-like,

a point behaving as a wave, which unless spotted by the godhead
must be said to be everywhere and nowhere at once: the science
of disappearance. I do not mean, guru, to break taboo or argue,
but why should my soul not be my body's moon,
visible only part-time, its dark side a hidden milieu?

And so adieu to you, guru—hereafter I must make-do with my soul
and my idea of my soul which, false or true, could it not be a sail
ready at any moment to let go of the boat and become itself
finally useless, and float? Like kudzu, guru, what it means to be
is to be of no use. If not truths, then at least truce?

Guru, bless my guess with yes.

## The Bargain

In the dream, we were walking, and we found on the ground
a dictionary of names. Paul, picking it up, turned, naturally,
to his own name, where he read *one who is easily broken, one
who will disappear*. Next Cato flipped to the page for *Cato*,
and found *one who is readily crushed, who will vanish*. He raised
his eyelids, bland as shower curtains, handed me the book, and it
was then I woke up, still pinched in this same skin. I dressed
quickly, slipped over my neck a length of black cord dangling
an ammonite, what I always wear on doorless days:
a Fibonacci spiral, a fossil's linked chambers whorling
like a galaxy or a thumbprint.

Himalayan-named *wheel of God*, cross-section of lobes
and saddles, of listening and fleeing, an ammonite reveals
to each either fear or salvation, if there is a difference.
For example, peasants of the Dark Ages dubbed the fossil
*a serpentstone*, seeing in its arc a petrified snake.
The Blackfoot Tribe beheld a buffalo curled and sleeping
in its helix, talisman for a journey or a hunt. Germans dropped it
in the milk pails of cows whose teats had hardened with refusal,
as if it were a magnet for letting go. But the wily ancient Greeks
would not settle on a single fear: under their pillows they slid
ammonites, amulets for peaceful dreams, hex against insomnia,
snake bites, impotence, and blindness.

This is why I wrap the scant and coiled weight around
my windpipe: because for 412 (plus or minus 2) million years
it has neither broken nor vanished. I bought it at the county fair,
part talisman, part fetish. Only four dollars it cost me, less than
three tickets to the Tilt-a-Whirl for Paul and me and Cato.

# Self-Portrait, with Vertigo

If my range of vision is imagined as a clock face,
it's toward eleven that I cannot tilt my head
without my inner ear shaking like a snow globe,
setting otoliths awhirl in a blizzard of dizzy.

The specialist calmly explained, *There's nothing to be
done. From now on, you simply don't look there.* At first
it was difficult to remember. I launched a private earth-
quake when reaching for horseradish on the top shelf.

Once from the window of a train I watched a crane
take flight, leftward leftward up, into an ocular orbit;
it was hours before I could escape. It hardly happens now;
the doctor was correct: I simply don't look there.

After all, who among us has not lost something small
and bone-like in a labyrinth we hadn't known was there?
A grief perhaps, or a memory, a longing banished long ago
to the fringes of our knowing, yet ever present in a corner

we are careful not to look toward. Here is what you get
if you turn to see: your head a gyroscope minus alleluia.
Here is what you get if you don't: your heart hidden
like the box you found beneath your father's stash of socks,

a cardboard coffer filled with milk teeth—yours and all
your sisters'—each open at one end like a feather, a broken
promise, like the ocean. Meanwhile your head's perched
atop your neck until some inner avalanche rolls it like a die.

Or rolls the world (less you) like a die. Like dying.

# Burning Aunt Hisako

Afterward we sifted through her ashes
with long chopsticks—one bamboo
and one willow, for this life and the next.

The furnace-keeper lifted bone by bone.
*Her ankle bone*, he tendered. *Her left thumb*.
A plate-shaped bone he named *her face*,

just before he smashed it into pieces
small enough to drop inside a dull bronze urn.
*What are we looking for?* I whispered

as we sifted. *From her throat, a bone
that's said to hold a seated Buddha*.
From Adam's rib to this, does at least one bone

from every body belong to someone else? Never
mind—what use are their own bone Buddhas now,
to Aunt Hisako smoldering on her slab,

to my mother's brother sealed beneath a hard
glittering snow? Bits of mica, memory
of fireflies—my own hand on my own throat—

of what use is this thirst for *things*
resembling other *things*, this endless trying
to wring milk from a two-headed cow.

## Letting Go of Letting Go

Only after we had already crossed it
did my husband tell me the name
of the old stone bridge in his hometown.
It was *The Thinking Bridge*.

A train to catch, I had no time for turning
back to where a thousand years ago
a monk had stood alone with his reflections
on the water. Between whichever two

anchored points his thoughts had been suspended—
like a life—they had not saved him. A hooded crane
flew low beneath the bridge and disappeared.
In the pocket of my coat, I touched the green stone

I'd been carrying concealed for nearly nine months
as if it was a charm, a child, a code: stone
for permanence, green for impermanence. Too late
to throw it from the bridge, I dropped it in the road.

# Cloud Mythology

Remus, Romulus and Cumulus were brothers, foster brothers. The first two were the by-products of the biologically confusing union of vestal virgin and God of War; thus it was not surprising they were bellicose babes. Abandoned on the River Tiber, they were rescued and suckled by a wolf. One day the wolf brought Cumulus home as well. He had fallen from the sky, but judging from his similar temperament the wolf had no doubt he was family. Cumulus was a fair-weather cloud, but under the right (or wrong) conditions he could produce heavy thunderstorms, not unlike his foster brothers' tantrums. One day Romulus killed Remus in a brawl over some land, or perhaps a woman. Cumulus was stricken in every droplet: Remus had been the one who'd taught him that with concentration he could spin tornadoes, with enough nasty thoughts he could spit hail. Romulus on the other hand had called him a windbag. Later Romulus disappeared in a violent storm, and a self-satisfied Cumulus was seen shortly thereafter ascending.

Once there were two brothers, Cirrus and Sirius. Actually Cirrus was more serious than Sirius, but he was also a cloud, so people took him lightly. To make matters worse, his name meant 'tuft or curl of hair,' which he resembled when he wasn't transparent. It's no wonder he was left out of the Egyptian Book of the Dead. "But Sirius was a *dog*," he cried in his rage at being overlooked. "Yes, but a faithful dog who was placed high in the heavens as a star." "But I'm a mass of ice crystals at the highest altitude reached by clouds. Just as sparkly, nearly as elevated," argued Cirrus. "Yes, but Sirius is the star where souls go when they leave the body." "No," said Cirrus sadly, "again you have gotten us confused." He would have rained to show his distress, but he wasn't a rain cloud.

Atlas and Stratus were brothers. As boys, or rather boy and water vapor, they were quite close, but as they reached adolescence, Stratus just sort of drifted off. Atlas, on the other hand, stayed close to home, maybe too close. Condemned by Zeus to plant his trapezoidal feet on the western edge of the earth and hold the heavens on his shoulders, what he was actually holding was mostly cloud, since that is what heaven is made of. In fact, he was holding mostly stratus clouds. Thus we got the phrase, "He ain't heavy, he's my brother," which isn't actually true. Clouds are heavier than you might think; so are brothers.

Columbus and Cumulonimbus were twins separated at birth by a mother who firmly believed in the good twin/bad twin dichotomy. She kept Columbus, who more closely resembled her, being human and all, and she abandoned Cumulonimbus, the thunderhead, to the skies. Columbus grew, unaware of his missing twin, yet he felt at a loss he couldn't explain. To his mother's grief, he left home to wander the globe looking for what, he didn't know. Out on the open sea, he could see for miles, driving his crew wild by steering towards storms. He didn't know what compelled him to do so, but it was this irrational habit that tossed his ships off course and brought him his fame. Still he felt empty. So he left the field of exploration to become a tornado chaser. He was closing in on truth.

Nemesis and Nimbostratus were sisters, equally misunderstood, as women with force often are. Nemesis was the executrix of fortune; this was her assignment from the gods. She pursued her delivery of justice according to what was warranted with exactitude and proportion. Nonetheless, humans, not wanting to accept responsibility for their own misdeeds, sneered at her and labeled her their worst enemy, an affliction upon men. Likewise Nimbostratus was maligned due to her, well, let's call it fecundity, which got her the nickname Nymphostratus, and worse. It wasn't fair. "I'm a rain cloud," she protested, "I'm *supposed* to nurture and nourish equally." In rage, she withdrew her gifts from the most crass of her slanderers, unlike Nemesis who continues to this day to visit her justice on everyone equally. And that is how we got deserts. As well as desserts, just desserts, I mean. And so reader, it would behoove you to remember: neither sister is out to get you.

two

## In Praise of the Candle Clock

In its way the candle clock was the most accurate timepiece ever
though it marked only intervals passing, its waxen column
melting down to the first gouged line—an hour elapsed—
then dissolving to the second—two hours gone—and so forth.

Over the stolid sundial its chief improvement was persistent vanishing
even on dark days, on dark nights, and indoors, its flame a contradiction
of illumination and immolation. Lacking interest in consensus
with the heavens, the taper treasured only span, measured not particular

nor point nor appointment. Here's what made the candle clock
a timepiece so precise: when time was up, there was no clock.
Collapse of candle mirrored the dark of time elapsed, all that is required
for human lapses and relapses. The borrowed beeswax was a clock in the way

the human body is, fixing time as disintegration, its function of self-
destruction the mark of Cain we recognize. We might claim
to identify instead with wick or flame, but it's the molten tallow
cooling sooner than expected whose downward flow we follow,

reminding us: as long as there is in this world a clock, we have no chance
of acting without a reason, no hope of such purity in being or in guttering—
beguiled, like piebald priests who spent candles to clock sermons, like tonsured
     monks
pausing their illumination only to calculate when it was safe, at last, to stop
     praying.

# A Sundial Explains the Uncertainty Principle

The piece of sundial that casts the shadow
is the *gnomon—one who knows*.
What it knows is that the visible rendering
of four dimensions erases light;
what's more, anything made to measure
gets in the way of what it reckons;
and knowing something without uncertainty
requires not knowing its conjugate pair:
place and momentum, time and energy—
the pairs not always what you'd expect.

In the Dark Ages, serfs scratched sundials
into the bottoms of wooden clogs.
To discern the hour, they went barefoot,
dusty shoes upended to catch the sun.
Heel-dark shadows fingered time on soles.
To not know this, they kept walking.
Soon city dwellers built timepieces freed
from the reins of all-knowing light.
They pretended not to notice the pendulums
swinging like legs on the march,
the gears clicking like clogs of peasants
across frozen fields, endlessly scavenging
for ungleaned wheat before winter snows
became the gnomon of the earth.

Now in your houses are digital clocks
engineered to hide the telltale ticking.
Instead, your spouses drum fast fingertips,
your adolescents crank up the bass.
You close your eyes against the shadows
only to hear the bright jackhammer
under the thin skin called your temples—
*tempus span*—meaning *timely space*:
a precarious spot where striking your enemy
yields a mortal blow. But who's
your enemy? If you don't know, take comfort
you do know his conjugate pair,
though it won't be obvious—maybe your neighbor,

or the month of April, or
your own shadow. Almost anything
casts a self-shaped shadow. You know this
one fact, but it will not help you. Just keep walking.

# On Getting Bifocals

*Here lies Salvino degli Armati, son of Armato of Florence,*
*inventor of the eyeglasses. May God forgive his sins. AD 1317.*
*—Memorial inscription as reported by Leopoldo del Migliore*

### 1. More Convex (near)

Tilt your head and what was
an almond tree becomes a twister's
verdigris. At any distance
another distance is smudged
in the eye's corner. Variable
vantage of a wasp, many-cornered
eye, for relief of time-
space collision apply bifocals.
You will, you are told, get used
to this polyhedrous panorama,
focal backflips like a filmstrip.
In middle age, the locus of focus
is bogus. Vision becomes
revision, glance shuffling
the cards your memory used
to. In theory, you were always ready
to collaborate with distance, as if
it was not a fact. In practice,
facts take practice, as plastic
the clock closes into a wink
with just a jut of your chin.

### 2. Centerline

Middle age, half an equal
sign, when near = far, both
useless unless unbraided.
Thank Franklin, Ben, father
(most likely, as seen from
this distance) of bifocals.
If he himself did not fashion
the first pair, he had them
made. You neither fashioned yours,

nor think of them as fashion, but
as fact, whatever that is. Don't
look now, the wind is
mating with the trees.
Another fact: you and Ben share
a hometown, share this pilgrimage
to presbyopia, failure to fix
your gaze anywhere without
convex disillusions. Or are they
illusions, oiled paper windows
through which prairie settlers could not see
summer making her gauzy getaway.

### 3. Less Convex (far)

A glass or globe filled with water,
an emerald, polished quartz:
all were ancient remedies
for ocular apostasy, known by Seneca
*the Younger*, and Nero, gladdened
by gladiators stepping out
of a fog. Blind gods, yes,
but no deities with glasses—
a manageable god is a dangerous god.
Later: spectacles, bifocals,
progressive lenses, penultimate
smudging of the line that erases
all smudges. In the meantime, praise
remembering. Praise forgetting. Praise
the ratio between them making the present
bearable. Are those birches reflecting
on the pond, or silver peeling
from a mirror's back? Praise the echo.
Praise bifocals, from all other possibilities
sieving only what you'd expected
to see.

## Ode to the Hourglass

The hourglass is the glamour puss in the world of timekeeping.
Even standing on her head she's all business and sex appeal,
simultaneous. *Live in the moment* is her mantra, and because
she offers no hard data, you do. She is a power lass, the hourglass,
a favorite among sailors, and not for what you think. It was
her equanimity they loved, her constancy across inconstant
weather and tempestuous seas. They chanted, *Let us sing
a ditty for the timepiece that's so pretty*, but what they
meant was, *Many thanks for the longitude revealed with
the lift of your eggshell petticoat.* Her comely shape
drives men to calculate which is why she needs no
numbers on her tumblers. *Fellas, it's all relative*,
she murmurs, her voice as smooth and cool
as finely powdered marble.

Lately she's been relegated
to the kitchen or the board game. Still,
when she kicks her ankles high above her shoulders,
you too go head over heels, fishing with your best line:
*There's nothing sexier*, you wink, *than the passing of time.*
She cartwheels, 1300 years of knowing it. And when she says *sexy*
she means *desperate*. Still, a gymnast of primness and suggestion,
she makes you for a minute, or three, forget the cargo that careens
your capillaries looping through the one-way valve you've come to call
your heart. No matter how many times you've seen her slide sideways
on her axis you still insist time flows in one direction, like you do,
lock step, all cause and effect, while she is of two everythings, or more,
and equally. That's why, when she grants you the dainty twist of her wrist,
you never ever know if she's waving good-bye to you or waving hello.

# The Invention of the Clock Face

~*The same structure in the brain for remembering the past
also imagines the future.* Thus the only credible clock
is the wind.

    ~The source of the sound of the tick of a clock
    is a mechanism called the escapement. Translating
    pendulum's swing into thrust of gear, it speaks
    lines into circles. Lines that you could escape from,
    circles that you can't.

        ~At first all clocks were faceless,
        their hours belled like cattle
        to caution us of their passing.
        It was the invention of escape-
        ment that made the face possible:
        the same drive, it was observed,
        could turn a dial with hands. And
        wherever there are hands there must
        also be a face for the hands to cover.

~Thus time came to be measured by angles between two hands, each with one
end tamped, like a shoulder, the other
in endless orbit, never reaching escape
velocity. By turns, they chase
and flee, reminding you
less of hands than of
handcuffs.         ~Each hand of a clock
            spins like a lasso, catching nothing
            again and again, circling like a rowboat,
            a rowboat whose sculler has dropped an oar.

    ~A clock holds its hands as cover, ashamed
    like any face valued chiefly for its symmetry, its angles.
    A clock pretends not to know: the function of a face
    is to be a front for the escapement, distraction for the inevitable.

~The ticking of a wristwatch
masks the shudder of a pulse beneath.
Ten thousand sepia moth wings.

Then slap of oar on water
like a hand across a face.
                    ~Listen, the wind is beginning to blow.
                    It says: Go ahead, drop the other oar.

## The Blind Man's Wife Makes a List of Words
## She Must No Longer Use

*Venetian blinds, blind alley, blindfold, eyelet, eyesore, eyes in the back of your head,*
*buckeye, bull's-eye, red-eye, naked eye, foresight, hindsight, oversight, insight,*
*bird's eye view, eyewitness,*
The guillotine is in the details. Observe
my husband failing gravity's pop quizzes
one by one, Pangaea dissolving beneath
his tread. Questions I do not ask him:
is it easier now, to believe in charm
quarks and muon neutrinos,
invisible lattice of matter we keep
slamming into? And crop circles,
do they seem more or less
like hoaxes, Braille letters thumbed
into the dirt for the eyeless
five-hearted earthworms to read
from beneath, a worship of wings?
His retinas in a patina of light,
his brown eyes as green as migration,
he quotes the mathematician Poincaré:
"Geometry is not true, it is advantageous."
*blind chance, blind spot, robbed blind, pull the wool over your eyes, blind drunk, blind*
*ambition, keep your eyes on the prize, can't believe my eyes, unsightly, sight unseen,*
*blindside, see red, see if I care, eye of the needle, evil eye, an eye for an eye,*
What's happening to him is biblical,
smitten by God's curse counted
among madness and astonishment of the heart.
In his hidden ribcage are all his five hearts
astonished? Blemished, say ancient prophets,
blocking their clandestine altar. Thanks, but
he doesn't need your forbidden veil, having become
his own. Until you're blind, there's no labyrinth
like the Holy Ghost. He's losing his sliver
of vision in a tarnish of vanish, his game
of hide-and-seek with the moon.
In life, as in math, whatever happens
happens at the boundaries, shatters like light
on fronds of ferns, splayed in the wind,
rising and falling like small green ribcages. No
matter: once you're blind, there's no labyrinth

like the Holy Ghost's ribcage.

*blind me with science, double blind, eyeball it, turn a blind eye, blind as a bat, see you
later, see a man about a dog, more than meets the eye, watch out, keep an eye on it, eye-
opener, sight-seeing, see the light, see eye to eye, the public eye, do it with my eyes closed,*

Things we don't need anymore: erasers,
masks, graph paper, fireflies. Definite
articles are useless now, or indefinite
ones—it's not clear which.
With nothing between the vanishing
point and the point of no return,
my husband twists into a Möbius strip,
membrane between outer and inner
flayed, a menagerie of one.
Now nothing he points to
changes. The hush of my camisole,
he says, slipping off my shoulder is
the sound of snow falling. Do not be
astonished: the signal-to-noise ratio
of falling is, like the speed, a constant.
One known thing. Consider gravity,
consider a vacuum. Consider blindness,
a special case of each, and by special
I mean, of course, limbo.

*blind date, love at first sight, second sight, stars in your eyes, only have eyes for you, blind
love, blind devotion, sight for sore eyes, see-through blouse, easy on the eyes, roving eye,
eye candy, bedroom eyes,*

One measure of a Japanese garden is
placement of elements: stones, lanterns,
boughs of pine. Between any three,
the gardener must see a triangle.
The visitor must not. Who gardens our bed
now the triangle between him and me
and my body is skewed, as in any holy
trinity one edge invisible: open side
of a triangle of geese flying south
to certainty, root of a fang bedded
in blood-colored gums? His origami eyelid
folds and unfolds into nothing
but what it is. Behind it he waits, subtracting
geometry from darkness to find fear.
Meanwhile, the corners of my treacherous eyes
spin figures that aren't there: dark legs

hoisting themselves over balconies, a torso
dangling from the eaves. When I turn to look,
there is nothing. This must be, I think,
*not* how my husband feels, but the opposite.
*the blind leading the blind, eye of the storm, no end in sight, drop out of sight, in the*
*blink of an eye, flying blind,*

# Portrait of a Clock as Repeating Decimal

The third hand, which is the second hand, is a one-armed bandit.
The second hand, which is the minute hand, plays an etude
for left hand only, in the lonely timbre of E flat minor's umber.
The hour hand augers crop circles cryptically out of ether,
augurs neither out of either, argues binary out of breathe.
1 face : 3 hands suggests a ratio best expressed as the tick
of repeating decimal: 0.33333333333333333333333333333333333333333333333333333
endless as three circles, relentlessly concentric
a census of facial tics, a subliminal echo
of pulse, thrum between bone and skin.
No wonder clocks make us squirm, as though waiting for the end
of a bad blind date, or for a bomb to detonate.
The ticking is the sound of one hand clapping.

# Processional

An even seam of ants can stitch a husk of katydid
to ether while sewing self to sidewalk.
Dots and dashes of belly and thorax
stream a coded message for Montana, for Milan,
spelling by exoskeletal abraxas a thread
of threnody. (365 is the secret number.)

Graph paper grasshopper, all green angles
and axis, is empty as a crinoline, silent
as a coffin's cacophony. (The password is
*Breathe*.) The living lift the dead in procession,
in possession of ever-pressing moment,
movement mindless and planetary,
a pinprick cortege unhitching its ardor for order.
(The secret color is invisible.)

If you describe the color green
to the color gold, gold will protest your illusion,
or at least your indiscretion. It knows
a secret: how we pretend not to notice
the days like a bucket brigade,
passing our bodies along.

## Three Views of Mars

Though I have spent most of today wiping my baby's bottom, raw from a bout of diarrhea, tonight we will wait until deep darkness, rouse the sick child and his pajama-clad brother, and go to the observatory to see Mars. I will hold my older son up to the telescope, praying that this time he won't swing it away from the red planet, toward the appalled graduate students who will have to reset it, not an inconsequential matter.

I'll say to my son, "Do you see the big red star?" and he'll answer, "I don't know." He's three; "I don't know" could mean "Yes," or "No," or "I have my eyes closed like last time." It might even mean he is already night-blind, the first symptom of retinitis pigmentosa, the disease blinding his father.

I will help my husband onto the footstool behind the telescope, guide his cheek to the eyepiece, but I won't ask if he sees anything. "Is it really red?" he'll want to know. I'll consider. It looks to me only slightly more orange than the other yellow-white stars visible. Red is the last color my husband lost before everything went monochrome. Except it was really purple he was seeing as red. "Yes," I'll tell him, "a vivid red."

My husband is not quite blind yet. His field of vision always narrowing, he sees as though through the center of a knot slowly tightening. These days it is like looking through the band of my wedding ring held about three inches from my face.

We will stagger back to the car in the darkness, the feverish baby slumped and dozing over my shoulder, the three-year-old hinged to my knee, my husband clamped to my free arm. We are like one grotesque organism, a lost and limping monster, an alien unequipped for life on Earth. I will narrate as we walk. "Curb in three paces, hydrant to the right, lone jogger heading straight at you."

After we put the boys to bed, my husband will lie down next to me and say, "The closest in 66,000 years. I'm so glad we didn't miss anything." Outside Mars is already receding, a pinhole of light getting ever smaller until it is gone.

## A Metronome is the Opposite of Wind

Wind launches the laundry, shakes hands
with a scarecrow, shuffles rust-edged petals

of dogwood, hungry for anything hung,
dangled, crucified. *Who do you*—or maybe

*Hoodoo you*, she calls, passing. The wind is
a woman, we say, when a thing disappears;

a man, when a thing is demolished.
I've come to the field today to be

away from metronome, clock, and door—
instruments of opening and closing, of doing,

undoing, redoing. The wind is no one's
instrument; it opens and opens, which is why

it cannot stay. Once you made me a gift
of a metronome, saying, *Without symmetry,*

*there'd be too much to desire.* What your rule forgets
is the human heart's four unequal chambers,

left of center. But its valves close and open,
its throbbing is even, metronome in give-and-take

with wind. Or vice versa. No one's wholly satisfied,
or wholly dispossessed, in this elliptical ruin of breath.

# Landlocked

Turns out I was wrong—the words *landscape* and *escape* don't share a root.
Instead *escape* is from the French for the cape you shed in your pursuer's hands
as you flee, while *landscape* first was Dutch, for the being-ness of land, a word
from the dyke-builders, culling land from sea: landship, like friendship and
kinship,

in the Masters' dark caves of thick paint. Nor, after all, are *landscape* and *escape*
opposites, antidotes, the solace I'd held on to. Turns out you can't slip off the
earth

like a cape, can't flee for someplace else unseen and scape-less. Could the
opposite

of *scape*, then, be *space*, that ever-expanding realm in which everything moves

away from everything else, flees, while I am still here, still life. The scapegoat
in the wilderness shares its root not with the *landscape* it roves about in,
abandoned,

fled from, laden with the sins of others thrust upon it like a cape, but instead is
rooted

with *escape*, though whose? Even when I die, dirt is where they'll bury me—land
is where I'll rest, or be said to rest, shrouded in its surface, my last-grasped cape
my body,

the sin-bound scapegoat I am tethered to, as space moves cleanly and facelessly
away.

# Night View from the Back of a Taxi

The skyscraper's amber-lit windows
are beads on a vertical abacus
reckoning the city's insomnia,
toting up, like photons, its sins.
Holes in the dark's architecture,
rectangular doppelganger of prayer beads
minus the turn and click of hope,
windows are the color of other, the density of hush.

I circumnavigate the city for hours, recalling
the scarecrow I'd confused with a crucifix,
my mother's bonsai heart.
Balanced on the seat beside me
is the bottle of eyebright you gave me,
saying *an herb for both memory and eyes*.
I took it, wondering: how can anything good for the memory
also be good for the eyes?

The taxi slows for a yellow—no, a red light.
Color is the Babel of the eyes. For example, in Ojibwe
there's a verb tense for what was going to happen
but didn't. As in, I was going to ask the driver to start homeward,
but then the light turned green. The city hides
its horizon, conceals its vanishing point. A stoplight's
three garishly made-up eyelids are each the fractal
of a planet you cannot fall off of.

three

# The Girl Whose Favorite Color is Eigengrau

*Eigengrau (German:"intrinsic gray"), also called Eigenlicht ("intrinsic light"), dark light, or brain gray, is the color seen by the eye in perfect darkness. Even in the absence of light, some action potentials are still sent along the optic nerve, causing the sensation of a uniform dark gray color. Eigengrau is perceived as lighter than a black object in normal lighting conditions, because contrast is more important to the visual system than absolute brightness. For example, the night sky looks darker than eigengrau because of the contrast provided by the stars. (from http://en.wikipedia.org/wiki/Eigengrau on 11/30/2012)*

*"Color is the place where our brain and the universe meet."*—Paul Klee

*"Color is an act of reason."*—Pierre Bonnard

# Pity the Girl Whose Favorite Color is Eigengrau

Pity the girl whose favorite color is eigengrau. She cannot say so without seeming to be pretentious. She is a lungfish, able to exist anywhere and thus at home nowhere, except in the dark which is lit by her consciousness although she cannot see that, and also cannot help but see it, and thus it is not the dark. The girl whose favorite color is eigengrau also has a least favorite color and it is eigengrau. This she also cannot say and for similar reasons.

## The Girl Whose Favorite Color is Eigengrau is Mocked by Those She Had Thought to Be Friends

The girl whose favorite color is eigengrau has a favorite road, edged on both sides by ancient trees that make in spring a pale tunnel, in autumn a patchwork canopy turning slowly threadbare, in winter a ribcage. The girl adores traveling this road even though it dead-ends at the hospital. One day, driving with friends on a cross street to her favorite road, the girl whose favorite color is eigengrau points and says, "That's my favorite road." Immediately one friend gestures at a rock and says, "That's my favorite rock," and another friend points to a stop sign and says, "That's my favorite stop sign." The girl whose favorite color is eigengrau says nothing, recalling to herself how Wittgenstein had written: "Imagine someone pointing to a place in the iris of a Rembrandt eye and saying, 'the walls in my room should be painted this color.'"

## The Girl Whose Favorite Color is Eigengrau Compares Words to Stones in a Japanese Garden

When she was young, the girl whose favorite color is eigengrau liked paint-by-numbers, though she never cared for connect-the-dots. This she recalls as she walks along a stepping-stone path through a Japanese garden. She has read that in certain parts of the garden the stones have been placed at awkward intervals for a slow and contemplative passage, while elsewhere stones have been laid evenly to encourage a natural gait. Still elsewhere the stones' placement suggests a hurried pace through where the garden is not yet finished, where it may never be finished. Darkness too, thinks the girl whose favorite color is eigengrau, changes the way we lope through it. Darkness, too, in some places may never be finished. And words, like stones in the darkness, are laid over here, haltingly, unevenly, and over there, as flowing and slick as gray paint.

## The Girl Whose Favorite Color is Eigengrau Thinks About Thinking

The girl whose favorite color is eigengrau reads that 95% of an average person's thoughts have been thought by that very person before, and thus are in effect recycled thoughts. She thinks, not for the first time, that this thing she has read cannot be true, and so researches it on the Internet, where she finds the same claim with different percentages, all of them over 90. The girl whose favorite color is eigengrau thinks that thinking the same thoughts again and again is like a blind man cleaning up broken glass.

## The Girl Whose Favorite Color is Eigengrau Laughs at an Inappropriate Joke

In her high school play, the girl whose favorite color is eigengrau doesn't have a speaking part, and this to her seems suitable. At practice one day she overhears a boy who does have a speaking role telling a joke. The joke is told backstage, between scenes, between friends. The boy says, "Imagine this: a one-legged man steps on your foot." The boy's friends hoot as, hopping on one leg, he lands on a friend's foot and says, "Pardon me for stepping on your foot." The girl whose favorite color is eigengrau turns away to hide her laugh. It is this turning away she recalls years later, when choosing a name for her cat, whose left side is black and whose right side is, symmetrically, white. This is how the girl whose favorite color is eigengrau comes to live with the cat named Schrödinger.

## The Girl Whose Favorite Color is Eigengrau Fails to Think Nothing

While taking deep breaths, as her meditation teacher has instructed, the girl whose favorite color is eigengrau practices thinking nothing, but instead ends up remembering contemporary artist Sara Genn, who said, "Having a favourite colour is like having a favourite lung." The girl whose favorite color is eigengrau takes a deep breath and again tries to think nothing, but this time instead ends up wondering if thinking nothing one time is the same as thinking nothing a previous time. A third time she tries to think nothing but this time starts to notice that failing to think nothing is not unlike seeing eigengrau where black should have been. The girl whose favorite color is eigengrau takes yet another deep breath and yet again tries to think nothing but instead begins to wonder if a lungfish has a favorite lung.

## The Girl Whose Favorite Color is Eigengrau Attends a Shuttle Landing

During graduate school, the girl whose favorite color is eigengrau dates an astrophysicist who wears brown corduroy. She considers telling him of her love of eigengrau; surely, she thinks (and not for the first time), an astrophysicist knows something about absolute dark, although having a human brain, he will not have ever seen it. Instead, she decides to break up with him. But before she can, he invites her to a shuttle landing and she says yes. They drive three hours into the middle of a desert where temporary bleachers inexplicably stand. The shuttle doesn't actually land here, but the girl whose favorite color is eigengrau hears a sonic boom as the shuttle reenters the atmosphere. Also, the sky ripples like water. Like water into which something has been dropped, and lost. The girl whose favorite color is eigengrau had never imagined such a thing in the sky. She recalls Wittgenstein, who wrote, "When dealing with logic, 'one cannot imagine' means: one doesn't know what one should imagine here." On the way home, the girl whose favorite color is eigengrau breaks up with the astrophysicist who wears brown corduroy.

## The Girl Whose Favorite Color is Eigengrau Considers the Word Eigenlicht

The girl whose favorite color is eigengrau prefers for her favorite color the name eigengrau to the other names offered—brain gray, dark light, and most especially eigenlicht, which suggests, she thinks, brightness. She thinks of the American illustrator Greg Parrish who said, "If time were a color, I bet it would be a tasteful off-white." She thinks of Leonardo da Vinci, who said, "Black is like a broken vessel, which is deprived of the capacity to contain anything." Time too seems to be deprived of the capacity to contain anything, thinks the girl whose favorite color is eigengrau. In the meantime, the cat named Schrödinger has had kittens: one black, one white, and two black-and-white symmetrically, like their mother. The girl whose favorite color is eigengrau names the kittens Parrish, da Vinci, Wittgenstein, and the cat named Schrödinger's Cat. The next day, the kittens are nowhere to be found, and the girl does not know if they are alive or dead, if they exist elsewhere or nowhere, or if they ever or never existed.

## The Girl Whose Favorite Color is Eigengrau Gets Married

The girl whose favorite color is eigengrau marries a blind man whose eyes are the color of a Rembrandt iris. She and her husband never discuss eigengrau in the same way that they don't discuss red and green and yellow. The girl whose favorite color is eigengrau knows that Wittgenstein responded to the assertion that "Light is colorless," with "If so, in the sense in which numbers are colorless." When her husband asks her what her favorite color is, the girl whose favorite color is eigengrau says, "Nine." "Galileo," she says, "was born on the same day da Vinci died."

## The Girl Whose Favorite Color is Eigengrau Plays an Etude for Left Hand Only

Although she is right-handed, the girl whose favorite color is eigengrau considers her left hand her favorite hand in the way a one-legged man favors his missing leg. She takes music lessons and insists on learning only pieces for the left hand only. This tradition includes sonatinas, gavottes, polonaises, and etudes, among others. The history of pieces for the left hand only began with the invention of the sostenuto pedal, which allows older notes to linger while new notes are being played, permitting the one-handed pianist the illusion of playing more notes at once than is possible. Because she has never mentioned it, the blind husband of the girl whose favorite color is eigengrau may not know that she plays with one hand only. She wonders if he can tell, but cannot ask him without *tipping her hand*, as the saying goes. Over 90% of her piano-playing time, the girl whose favorite color is eigengrau wonders.

## Pity Not the Girl Whose Favorite Color is Eigengrau

The girl whose favorite color is eigengrau attends a lecture on Japanese poetic forms. There she hears about the *jisei*, the Japanese death poem, a traditionally short poem meditating on death, the ephemerality of life, and other related topics. The girl whose favorite color is eigengrau cannot think of any unrelated topics. When she returns home after the lecture, she sits on her sofa, the cat named Schrödinger curled in her lap, and writes her own *jisei*.

The mind is a gray wash over a field of black
but in the body's absence, the mind will either be
a blackness in a field of blackness or
a light in a field of light, and is there,
wonders the mind, any difference.

## Pity Not the Blind Man Who Has Married the Girl Whose Favorite Color is Eigengrau

Four elements are needed to create a silhouette, reads the girl whose favorite color is eigengrau: a light source, an obstruction to that light, a surface to receive the shadow, and a medium for recording the shadow's shape. She has a light source (a lamp), a receptive surface (butcher paper rolled out on the floor), and a medium (black paint). What she needs is an obstruction. First she tries the cat named Schrödinger, but she won't stay still, neither on her black side nor her white. Next the girl leads her blind husband to where he obstructs the light. "What are you doing?" he asks. "Drawing," she says. "Drawing what?" How do you explain a shadow to a blind man, wonders the girl, not for the first time. "You know when it's cold outside but warm inside and condensation forms on the window?" "Oh," says her blind husband, "you are drawing the window's tears." The girl frowns. "Its ablutions," she corrects. Her blind husband hears the word *blue* in the word *ablutions*; he doesn't know *blue* but he does know *the blues*, so he begins to whistle a tune. "Quiet please, I'm concentrating," says the girl whose favorite color is eigengrau, though she is only tracing a shadow.

# four

# The Book of the Edge

In daylight wall is fact. Roof is art-
ifact, vestige of first human-hewn structures,
which were only roof, all loose suture, even then
as functional as a fontanel in keeping darkness
out. Or in. On the roof at night raindrops
unmake themselves violently.
There is so much chaos even order
is made of it. Even fossils have electrons,
along the cusp spinning. Hubble redshift
at the universe's edge is the ultimate marginalia:
proof all things move away from their centers.
Another dark calculation for the halo-less,
the seraphs sans serif, all wall and no roof.

In daylight words are walls are fact.
But come night, come even-
tide we remember the word *invisible*
can be written down. *Silence* too
betrays: anyone can speak of it, so fact
at night is roof, ancient marginalia.
Like electrons. Like angels. There's so much history
even night is made of it. And walls. It's why,
numb as numbers, we still burnish the urgent stained glass
of forgiveness, letting through light but not fact.
As in, history is rain but raindrops are facts,
relinquishing their edges, like all facts,
when they run into a roof, a human edge.

## November Nocturne

Even planets turn away from the easement of light
sometimes. Night's a rehearsal for the orb
and distance of winter, its map-unmaking
and its unmap-making, its failure to ravel
wander from resist. All night the night
sounds like children not breathing. I am afraid
of a thing and its opposite: leaving and not,
subject unspecified. The curtain stirs
though the window is closed. Stars flash
like bees abandoning the hive, humming a lullaby
in drone, in monotone but with the Doppler effect
of a death mask, coming right at you, wind
pulsing around the edges because there is
no mouth-shaped hole, no eye-sized emptinesses.

## Self-Improvement Project #4

Days shorten until landscape = curfew.
In an alphabet unfit for lilacs, for orphans,
spell your given name, spell *loss*. Passing
headlights trace two of four bedroom walls
and vanish, or appear to vanish. Sit where,
when they come, they are at eye level.
When they don't come,
that's also at eye level.

# Possessed

To have and to hold—
the expression of possession is
the apostrophe's catastrophe.
We lust to master mass
the way a grackle grooms its luster.
We thirst to tame time
despite the known futility—
our antidote's to praise
the camera's utility
as pixilation's titillation
commemorates commodity.
The bodily's our gimmick,
as much as we can stomach.
In certain societies—the primitive—
the grammar of possession's
parsed and parceled as alienable
and inalienable, the latter
including body parts and kin,
as if by merely staying
intact and / or in touch (ouch!)
we win. As if anti-matter's
not the Lost Tribe of quantum physics.
*Omnium gatherum*, zero-sum game,
like moths about a flame,
like a nine-fingered man—
(inalienable be damned)—
possession is nine-tenths of the law,
a nine-fingered light-fingered man
in the dark and when he shakes *your* hand
count your fingers, count your sheep
as you slide possessions wide
and deep, as many as you can,
between your body
and the big big sleep.

## The Puppet

A hand wants a puppet.
What a hand really wants
but cannot have is a mouth.
A puppet has a mouth, small
and ineffectual but nonetheless.
A hand that has a puppet
has a mouth, or access to one.

A mouth, on the other hand,
doesn't want a hand.
If a mouth had a hand, it knows
the hand would cover it.
Then the mouth would need a puppet
with its throatless hand-hewn mouth
and its tiny malevolent fists.

## The Daughter-in-law, Newly Pregnant, Considers
##     the Water Cycle

Water in the bucket takes
the shape of bucket and
the river is not bereft.

Water in the jug, the cup,
takes the shape of jug, of cup.
The clouds are not bereft.

Edge to center. Puddle
to vapor to sky. Droplet,
rivulet, droplet.

Do not pity water
its ancient edgelessness.
From a holy highway of birds
rain thinks of you as a souvenir.

# Thistle

This is thistle.
Bus is bustle.
Kiss is castle.
If only.

A gorilla mask.
A glial mask.
A Galileo mask.
If only.

Cradle, not cruel.
Fable, not fool.
Riddle, not role.
If only.

Art is atlas.
Past is palace.
This is thistle.
This only.

## Self-Improvement Project # 5

There is no boat the rain will not ride,
even one afloat on a sea that is not numbered,
one slung between waters like a household between secrets.
A mariner's harmonica runs like a frayed rope through his hands.
Point by point, how long it takes for separation in the mouth.
Ritual involves tilt: habit is nourished anxiety. And the hurly-burly
of regret is two folded pieces of any bed I lie in. Did I tell you
how repetition soothes me? I did, yes, of course I did.

five

# The Function of the Comma is to Separate

One function of the comma is to separate items in a series. For example: In this room are a bed comma you comma me comma and a clock ticking overly loudly period

One function of the comma is to separate two or more independent clauses joined by coordinating conjunctions, as in: You are sleeping soundly comma whereas I am contemplating commas period

One function of the comma is to separate adverbs and short parentheticals that are not essential to the meaning of a clause, as when John Keene wrote: Open quote Desire is comma among other things comma a function of repetition ellipsis period close quote

One function of the comma is to separate adjectives that directly and equally modify or describe the same noun. For instance: The clock in this room is loud comma relentless comma repetitive comma annoying comma repetitious comma and comma among other things comma slow by three minutes period

One function of the comma is to separate alternative or contrasted coordinate phrases, such as: My desires are to be awake with you comma or to be asleep beside you comma not awake beside your sleeping form period

One function of the comma is to separate nonrestrictive modifiers, as in the following example: This night comma which is seeming to last forever comma is about to be punctuated by the destruction of this damn clock exclamation point

One function of the comma is to separate information about the source of a quotation from the quotation itself. For instance: John Keene wrote comma open quote Desire is comma among other things comma a function of repetition ellipsis period close quote

One function of the comma is to separate dates, geographical places, numbers, personal titles, direct addresses, and brief interjections from the body of a sentence. For instance: My darling comma your closed eyelids are two commas hanging between us period When you turn away from me in your sleep comma my love comma the curve of your back is comma among other things comma like a comma that separates us period

One function of the comma is to separate appositives that are not essential to the meaning of a sentence, such as in: The function of the comma comma the most irritating punctuation mark ever conceived other than the exclamation point comma is to separate period But I repeat myself ellipsis period

One function of the comma is to separate preceding prepositional phrases from the main clause of a sentence. For instance: In the morning comma or when you awaken comma whichever comes first comma my darling comma I will read to you the words of John Keene comma which are comma open quote Desire is comma among other things comma a function of repetition ellipsis period close quote It will be comma my love comma among other things comma as if you were hearing this for the first time period

# The Essence of Evanescence, or Vice Versa

Wind is its own cargo,
not the flotsam of blossoms,
not the pastiche of trash.

Trees may be forsaken
of acorns but wind is not
a centrifuge for foliage,

not a portico for vertigo,
and night's no indigo embargo
of light. Stillness, when it comes,

is no absence of violence,
no thrum of nothingness.
Less is meaning:(less)

and morning is not more.
Wind does not begin
nor does it flash a shadow.

A shadow is not cargo,
is not a block(age) to be
hoisted across the horizon,

which is no finish line.
Endings and beginnings
are not strangers, and the wind,

the wind does not unwind
from its invisible spool,
its centerless center.

And if you unmoor
before I do, if your cargo
goes to flotsam first,

what is not wind,
not night, not shadow,
will also be not me.

## Still Life in My Garage

The day the body of my good guitar
begins to resemble the pinched lips
of the symbol we all agree means
eternity, arpeggio of tundra, I carry it
out to my garage where the vagaries
of weather and ambience will do it no good.

Passing washers and wing nuts sorted
into once-empty jars on the workbench
I wonder, what if the ancient Atomists
were right? What if each object is busy
beaming streams of tiny images of itself
in a bid to be seen by the black hole
in someone's unforgivably blue iris?
As if end*less* equaled hope*ful*. Just in case
I find the only picture of myself
I've ever liked and bury it where
no one will ever find it. I had
the only copy.

Afterwards, I hang the shovel back
on the nail, above the carpenter's level
with its little bubble
caught like a secret in its throat.
It's only ever been asked a single question
as if that's all a firm grip on equilibrium
is good for. Or maybe it's a suggestion box
with only one admonition:
Look to the space where something is
missing. Or perhaps there's no good reason
it's also known as a spirit level.

Sometimes you come out of the house
to check on me, all blue-eyed and permanent.
The problem is, whenever any three
of the two of us get together, the walls
loosen, porous as birds' nests.
The ax heads glint and clink.

After you leave, I take garage door opener
in hand, raise and lower the horizon, again
and again, repeating aloud so that only I can hear,
words beginning with *no*:
nomadic, November, nocturne, north.

# Favorite Apples of the Presidents

*Newtown's Pippin, Rhode Island Greening, Spitzenburg, Black Twig*:
these were the favored fruits, in order, of Washington, Franklin,
Jefferson and Jackson, though some argue Jefferson esteemed more
the *Pippin* and Ben Franklin wasn't a president. Adams swilled cider,
while documents have Madison requesting the pie, which Lincoln
was also rumored to have fancied. For Van Buren, it was Dutch Apple Cake.

When I mouthed the words *Crow's Egg, Faust's Winter, Seek-
no-Further*, my husband remarked, "You shouldn't choose an apple
for its name," by which he meant, "You could never be the President."
My husband's top three: *Belle de Boskoop* (with a smirk),
*Slack-My-Girdle* (another smirk), and *Canadian Spy* (this time
with an all-out guffaw.) He will never be President either.

The *Bottle Greening* grows on a hollow-trunked tree in which
work gangs once stashed their bottles—more executive under-
achievers. But let's not talk of disappointment, of *Jelly Heart*,
of *No Bloom* and *Sink Hole*. William Tell, compelled to shoot
a fruit from atop his son's head, was aiming at what: a *Fired Sweet*,
a *Sweet Neverfail,* a *Crack*? Black Plague closed Newton's school,

so he dawdled in the garden where a falling *Flower of Kent* revealed
to him a law: Everyone falls, even Presidents. Speaking of which,
Eve too in a garden clutched an apple, perhaps a *Maiden's Blush*,
a *Gloria Mundi*, or maybe a *Fall Queen*. In orchards you will find
a *Magog*, but no Gog. *Jewel Smoker, Greasy Ball, Knobbed Russet*,
ugliest apple ever—all have been somebody's lunch. What do you need,

an *Aspirin*, a *Leather Jacket*, a *Transcendent Crab*? Forget apple scabs,
coddling moths, fire blight: there is an apple for everyone, not just Presidents,
thanks to wild seeds scattered across ancient Eurasia by the brown bear.
(Scattered by their scat? snorted my non-running mate, electoral college
dropout.) Did you, too, think things would be different, more *Glowing Heart*
and less *Grizzle Strain Shockley*? My secret is One-sided, *Two Tone*,

*Stump the World*: I never wanted to be President. In my mind
I was juggling three apples, pleased with their heft as they smacked
my imaginary palm and wheeled back into orbit. When I could no longer

picture my fist's ghost unclenched, I thought the apples would tumble
or turn to ash. Instead they kept circling, swarming without me,
like fireflies, like electrons: *Red Torque, Burning Green, Nonesuch.*

## Other People's Lives

Fewer facts than a tombstone
tree rings reveal. Wedding rings, too,
are stingy with details, data-vague.

They say nearly nothing
so as to avoid telling lies like a map,
which (just to have something to say)

pretends to know where, exactly,
water laid a hand on land.
As if it happened just that once.

Like all circles, a ring speaks
to only itself, repeating
secrets in a silent gold language.

You, of course, argue: Trees
aren't conscious, not even
mobile—there's not much

to know. In silence I spin
my gold band over the table
between us like a coin.

Headless, endless, which way
it pitches betrays precisely
nothing. Around the spool

of countable others, my mind winds
one more day of marriage,
rubbed thin and faint

as a date in the family Bible.
Greetings from a year without rain,
from the second most bitter winter.

Greetings from circles within circles
on the surface of a lake where
something small and contained once vanished.

## Knot Sonnet

My heart is a drawer crammed with postage stamps,
a two-strand shroud hitch waiting for an occasion.
You, on the other hand, have somewhere tomorrow to be.
The hour we awake will be the lead goose in a vee

flying southward. The second hour will be the first pair
of geese behind it, and so on, a widening space between
each next brace of birds as the day passes. In this metaphor,
we are not the geese, you and me. We are the people, grounded,

who, hearing the geese cry, glance up and think how
like a ribcage they sail through the air, beating, but say
nothing of it—a sailmaker's eye splice, which can't bear a load,
an open-hand knot best suited for ropes of unequal dimension.

It's not too late: I could hide your alarm clock in the lilac bush.
I could pour buttermilk in your good pair of shoes.

# Regretfully Yours

Who knows a burden better than a willow?
I do, who beckoned you to share with me my pillow.

Who knows a candle better than its tallow?
I do: you subsume me and yet know I will follow.

Who knows a closed fist better than a lasso?
I do, I—whose torque is centered in your torso.

Who knows a curtain better than a window?
I do, whose fate is as certain as a widow's.

Who knows murmuration better than a starling?
You do, who murmur to all the women, *Darling*.

Who knows a murder better than a warrior?
You, who find my ardor to be nothing more than error.

Who knows the netherworld better than a mourner?
Who knows a mirror better than a mirror?

## Tide Lines

The Moon last night eyed everything not nailed down—
in particular the seas, loose change in the planet's pocket.
                        The Moon tonight is a fist, breaking
with its light the black glass of my window, which is rectangular
like the holes we dig in this spherical planet in which to lay
our dead.
                The Moon has slipped, tonight, into a skimpier costume,
a template busy erasing itself. Here's what you said before you left:
*The closer to the water one lives, the more windows*
                *one will need.* Memory is not a window.
                                Once we believed the Moon
was Earth's doppelganger, turning like a lathe, sparking stars.
                Now I wonder, *how long until the sum of the parts ceases*
*to grieve for the whole?* Memory is a fist, suitable
for clutching and for punching, the two pantomimes of desire.
                                Nights the Moon is amber-bright,
I envy dirt. Nights the Moon is amber-dark I wade into waves
as far as my sacrum, flaring from the Latin for *sacred.*
                The Moon, too, is sacred tonight, girdled in a habit of light
                she cannot keep.
                        Now the sea spiral-spindles, ragged geometry
of gear-crush, excess of ritual, while the Moon winks in my window,
ever phosphorescent (light without heat).
                                She is the mapmaker's blind spot,
flirting with his memory until he inks a link between continent and brine,
a permanence where there's only quicksilver slide and verge.
                The Moon is as false as water. As the idea of desire, which is a whole,
while desire itself has never been the sum of anything, like a window
                just before a fist shatters it.

## The Secret to Keeping Secrets

Secrets as intricate as orchids rarely last.
One that cannot be named in seven words or fewer
will not stay a secret, or it will not stay at all.
Ordinary shame is not scarlet, like hibiscus or
a tanager, but the color of dried-up honeycomb—
rows of cells bleached almost yellow, fled from,
thin walls dividing the threat of nothingness
into bearable portions, like a calendar.

This is not a fable but a fact: wherever the color yellow
forgets to erase itself, a secret slowly comes undone.
In a mangrove, amid every fist-sized clump of green
there is a single yellow leaf, repository for the salt
the entire plant absorbs. Under the scaffolding
of a skull-colored shell hides the deep cadmium yellow
of yolk, sensing the very first secret, while autumn leaves
strain to master the last, yellow emptied of honey,

emptied of salt. Each secret is its own planet,
and in the original Greek *planet* meant *a wanderer*.
Driftwood. A way of being elsewhere, else one, less
self, parceled. Finally, every shame is this: *I can't be
what you want*, or vice versa. Why do we secretly love
our secrets? Because they are one-third marginalia,
one-third magnolia. This is true of *both* kinds of secrets:
the ship in the bottle, *and* the bottle in the ship.

## Exit Strategy: Pantoum

As soon as I can get myself together, I'm moving far away
from this factory of uncertainty. Here I'm always on the wrong end
of stigmata. Here the fractals of fact are to me as useful
as a quiver of arrows to an out-of-work glassblower. Color photos

of this factory of uncertainty are always on the wrong end
of factum, where $y = x$. For example, even Mason jars have haloes.
Even to quiver is an error for an out-of-breath glassblower. A color photo
is overkill for remembering cinders in the snow, balance of fantasy

and friction, where why $=$ exit, for example. Even Mason jars have holes,
exact fractures etched across the glass of existence. Never mind. Forgetting
is overkill for remembering. Cinders in the snow balance fallacy
with vanishing. Point the lonely way out of this one-mirror town, with its

exact fractures switched for the gloss of having never existed. Mind forgetting—
it's the last chance for salvation. I must try harder to blend in
with vanishing points: the only way out of this bone barrier is down. With its
maps of the infinite, its alphabets of silence, easement is the why

but what's the past tense of salvation? I must try harder to blend in
with stigmata, until the fractals of fact are to me as useful
as the mapped and infinite alphabet of the silent treatment. That is why
as soon as I can get myself together, I'm moving far away.

## If E Is Not for Eternal Love, What's It For?

So I follow you around, repeating your every utterance.
So what. You say my behavior is childish. I say
it's an opera of geometry. You say *Go away*. I say
I can't—we're of the same fractal, ragged copies
of various magnitudes, like a coastline, self-similar
at any distance. You say *Choose a farther distance*.
You say you'll call the cops. I say they can't arrest a shadow,
they can't lasso an echo. You say you can't believe
you were ever married to me. I say pendulum, metronome,
ear worm. I say repeating decimal. I say E is for echolalia.
I motion the audience of all our past selves. Everybody now:
E is for echolalia!

# A Pilgrim's Guide to Chaos in the Heartland

## 1. Road Trip

*It's a good idea to collect as much entropy*
*as possible before using a system.*
*——Jon Callas, cryptographer*

Because the horizon is not a number line,
because distance is an absolute value,
I use the atlas as an *I Ching*, a rune,
my calculations point to the Midwest,
as good a place as any.

Here in the disappe5aring prairie
I finally understand
how some infinities can be larger,
others smaller; how certain endless
quantities move closer to no end
faster than others.
Aleph Null—countable though infinite:
grass, sun, treelessness.
Aleph One—uncountable and infinite:
dust, wind, fire. The distance
between here and God.

And this I did not expect,
that the lon7eliness would be countable.

My son wants a tumbleweed for a pet,
now one is buckled in the back seat.
What a clever boy, choosing to love
a thing already dead and rootless.

At the motel, he watches me
lower the blinds against
the white noise, the presence
of all possibilit5ies in the night.
*It's such a lovely dark, Mama,* he says.

## 2. Devices of Chance

*Definition of Randomness: an inexplicable*
*misfeature; gratuitous inelegance.*
——www.gopher.quux.org:70

Two Defi4nitions of Randomness, Each Necessary but Not Sufficient:
    Numbers in a string are random if they cannot be expressed in an2y
    shorter form.              *But that is just poetry.*
    Numbers in a sequence are random if there is no patte6rn to them.
               *Is that unbel5ief or its absence?*

Ways to Generate Randomness/Pseudorandomness:
    throwi2ng dice, casting lots, flipping coins, d9rawing balls from hoppers,
    drawing straws, picking num0bers from 1 to *x*, playing rock/paper/ scissors,
    consulting random number tables, spooling algor9ithms through computers.
              *getting out of bed in the morni7ng*

A Short History of Dev7ices of Chance:
    Casting lots (ancient beyond history): object1s, cast to the earth, or into a
    recepta0cle and then drawn out—pebbles or dice, nuts or barleycorn, tw9igs,
    bones, coins, cards, yarrow sticks, precious gems. Once believed to reveal
    the will of god(s).

    D3ice (circa 2750 B.C., ancient Mesopotamia/the Indus Valley): fashioned
    from clay and passed through fire, dotted with pips mu8ch as today's.

    The astralagus (earlier than 1320 B.C., Egypt): dice-like bones with four
    fac9es, each different in shape.

    The quincunx (1823-4, Sir Francis Dalton, cousin to Darwin): the theory of
    errors m3odelled by pellets, dropped through a vertical maze of pins, landing
    in a bell shape that echoes the no9rmal curve.

*The ancients, too, wanted to live as though there wasn't enou1gh randomness in life, as*
*if it had to be sought out like a buried fam3ily secret, or something feral; as though it*
*wouldn't come looking for you in the night.*

    These days we know the sources of pure randomness are few. We measu5re
    cosmic ray flux, light emiss4ions from trapped mercury molecules, thermal
    noise from resistors, the decay of radioacti8ve material.
              *Trapped. Re9sist. Decay.*

## 3. Grassla6nds

*And Aaron shall cast lots upon the two goats;*
*one lot for the Lord, and the other lot for the*
*scapegoat....And the goat shall bear upon him*
*all their iniquities unto a land not inhabited:*
*and he shall let go the goat in the wilderness.*
—Leviticus 16: 8, 22

We haven't pass7ed another car all day,
j6ust the grasses undulating,
the winds ululating,
oceans of air drow749ning us.
In every dir7ection
the startling sameness—
easy to get lo3st,
imp4ossible to be lost.

Here in the New W4orld
eve8ryone wanders.
                    39787637
Fold the nation in half
le9ngthwise, endwise,
and the intersectio1n,
the pivot point, the spot
wher4e the map would crack fi3rst,
dead center, bla9ck hole,
is not far from here.            0

Perha6ps from that spot, south76westerly,
a tornado is h2eaded this way—
a conic7al tumbl3eweed,
a vortex, an altar,
a lot cast65 on the plains
5touching down here, ta9king
this one, leaving that one.
The sky turns briefly gre07en,
e9xplodes with missi9ves of ice,
the soun9d of ten thous58and waterfalls,
white noise, maskin7g our sounds,
chaff in the whirlwind40440.

Enter pure ran11domness:
708015impossible to be
lost; where pointle7ssness
is the po36int.

## 4. C7ounting Backwards

*White noise frequently isn't.*
　　　　—Jon Callas, cryptographer

05181261
　　The Tall08 Grass P5rairie States:
　　Nebraska, th0e Dakotas, Oklahom3a, Texas, Wisco5nsin, Missouri, Kans1as...
　　Staring at the para6llel rows of parallel 01 cornstalks, I remember that over
　　h14alf of all Americans liv7e in the State in which they were born640.
　　　　　　　*Behi3nd me, my son begins co8unting backwards.*

　　Co2mmon Uses for Counting Bac36kwards:　　　　　9684996263
　　　　to test for a6ging-related declines, dyslexi6a, and, in Texas, drunk dr3iving; to
　　901272increase concentrat4ion, to fa9ll asleep, in meditation; to hei8ghten
　　anticipation, as in annou9ncing beauty pageant winner8s or rocket launches
　　　　　　　*to connect w7ho you are with where you are*

　　　　　　　　　176833
　　How to Dis6tinguish a Child from 6an Adult:
　　　　For a child, countin06g backwards is as easy as counting for76ward9s.
　　　　An adult says5, *Anythi3ng could happen,* but is surpr7ised when it does. Or
　　　　doesn't; the future as 8unsure as the past. 7173Co4unting backwards is
　　　　impossible: betw10een any two number4s there are infinitely 07many more.
　　　097　　　　　　　*Counting forwards is worse.*

　　How to Tell if You Are A M32athematician:
　　　　If you thin2k rand7omness is desirable and too rar5e, like rubies; if you chase6
　　　　8entropy, like a butter33fly once thought to be extinc50t, you are a 036434
　　　　mathematic8ian.7652
　　　　　　　　86357

　　If you think r4andomness is as ubiq01uitous and welcome as dust, t3he
　　common cold, tract housin5g; if you would run9 from entrop8y if only there
　　were an6ywhere to run, you are no34t a mathematician.
　　　　　　　*Over half of all America6ns are not mathematicians.*
　　　　　　　　　73548768095909

1173929274
　　　1705

## 5. Crop Circles5

*There are several ways not to walk in the prairie,*
*and one of them is with your eye on a far goal. . .*
—William Least Heat Moon

Left, r9ight, straight—
each cros5sroad seems mome9ntous
yet insignificant. I                                69572
have lon4g since lost
3360699        the at5las, let go fistfu3ls
of yarrow sticks7 out the wi6ndow
of the8 rental car, like dan54delion
dander in the dry w2ind, cosmic                              5116877121
03101ray flux, lig04ht
radiating from som8ething trap6ped.
                                                        128

I am c8oming to the Am3erican m44id-
point, the 056epicenter,
0111668014groun9d zero, the cal4m                      76867
8at the eye of the s94torm.
Colle8cting entropy 155as I go.

Nowh7ere I have ever been            0100
is any different fro6m 2here.                              5023760
The buffa4lo grass and wild bergamot,
spiderwort la83sting only a day0858—
the 03prairie could be a latticed cit8y,
2962ragged mou2ntain, roofless de4sert, or 04020082
what it is.

I am b5ecoming th8e center of some circ5le,
all p9oints equi05distant from72 me,
interc2hangeable. I a2m zero-
ing in on random355ness.
                    4037206361                      2916650842268953
                533476435080
My so4n has said noth19ing
for fi3fty-three miles3.
In the re6arview mirr792or
I see him asle533ep,

his f3ace pressed 4into the tumb5leweed          093032320902560159
    I will have to soo7n let go
019like a scapegoat in the wil4derness.
                    2428426290833              68353

## 6. 015Random N6umberTab8le

*We know what randomness isn't,*
*not what it is.*
*——William A. Dembski*

8133988511199291703106010805455718240635303426148679907439234030973285269776020205165692686657481873053852471862388579635733213505325470489055357548284682870983491256247379645753035296477835808342826093520344352738843598520177671490568607221094055860970934335050073998118050543139808277325072568248294052420152775567851834529963406288980831374670078184754061068711778178868540200865075840136766679519036476493296091106299594673488751764969918260892893785613682 ***It*** 34783411365481174174685095058047769747303957186402181654480124356351772708015453182237421115782531438553763743509981777402772144323600210455216423796286026556991626803662522914836936872037662113990944005641809893205051422568514464275678896297788225438214598914991452368479276864616283554947508992337089200488033694598269403685870297341355314033340420508234144104819498515747954329791 ***is*** 26575576004088122222064131255073742111000204012074697966448943928707258156360649329165053448440219525634365177082072073179061196904462645747774519243372965394595934258260527154744526695270799535936783848823961011833211594669455728573678975438154622444319119042592929274597342481162139734408721168684876703071120592570146670235237831 ***a*** 77320889838935914162625229663055228256204493524947524633824458625102561962793356533712472005499765464051881599611963896546928239123287 ***lovely*** 9529359631530726898093543335135462779745002490339333598080839145427268428360949700130212489278565201064609092286772814407793910836477 ***dark*** 06174258852360139413217959787379252410556707007867431715785394118386923461406201174520415956600018743924239711896338195654143001758753794041921585666743680684962852074515514938194760724643667945435904790033208266954194864319943616810851648888155301540354560501451176980862482645240284044499908896390947340735441318803318516232419415094989435485818869541994375487304380951004069638270774201512338725016252989462461171797524914071961282966986 10 25